Soccer in Central America

By
Mike Kennedy
with Mark Stewart

NORWOOD HOUSE PRESS

Norwood House Press, P.O. Box 316598, Chicago, Illinois 60631

For information regarding Norwood House Press,
please visit our website at: www.norwoodhousepress.com or call 866-565-2900.

Photo Credits:
  All interior photos provided by Getty Images.
Cover Photos:
  Top Left: Topps Trading Cards.
  Top Right: Ned Dishman/Getty Images.
  Bottom Left: Martin Rose/FIFA via Getty Images.
  Bottom Right: The Upper Deck Company.
The soccer memorabilia photographed for this book is part of the authors' collections:
  Page 10) Figueroa: Panini.
  Page 12) Bailey: Panini; Gonzalez: SV Records & Videos; Fonseca: Nuestro Diario;
        Guevara: The Upper Deck Company.
  Page 13) Ruiz: The Upper Deck Company; Figueroa: Topps Trading Cards; Romero: Authors' Collection;
        Pappa: The Upper Deck Company.

Designer: Ron Jaffe
Project Management: Black Book Partners, LLC
Editorial Production: Jessica McCulloch
Special thanks to Ben and Bill Gould

Library of Congress Cataloging-in-Publication Data
    Kennedy, Mike, 1965-
    Soccer in Central America / by Mike Kennedy, with Mark Stewart.
        p. cm. -- (Smart about sports)
    Includes bibliographical references and index.
    Summary: "An introductory look at the soccer teams and their fans of
countries in Central America. Includes a brief history, facts, photos,
records, and glossary"--Provided by publisher.
    ISBN-13: 978-1-59953-443-5 (library ed. : alk. paper)
    ISBN-10: 1-59953-443-6 (library ed. : alk. paper)
    1. Soccer--Central America--Juvenile literature. 2. Soccer teams--Central
America--Juvenile literature. I. Stewart, Mark, 1960- II. Title.
    GV944.C375K36 2011
    796.33409728--dc22

                                        2010044554

Manufactured in the United States of America in North Mankato, Minnesota.
170N–012011

Contents

Words in **bold type** are defined on page 24.

Goal! Guatemala scores.

Where in the World?

Central America is made up of the seven countries between Mexico and South America. There is water to the east and west. Mountains run down the middle. There are soccer **leagues** everywhere.

Once Upon a Time

Soccer has been a popular sport in Central America for 100 years. In ancient times, people played a game called "Tlatchtli." It looked a little like volleyball and a little like soccer.

Gilberto was a top player for Honduras in the 1980s.

Players wave to the fans at Cuscatlan Stadium.

At the Stadium

The biggest stadium in Central America is Cuscatlan Stadium in El Salvador. It was the first stadium in the region to have a large video screen. Central American players love to play games there.

Town & Country

Maynor Figueroa of Honduras is a star on both sides of the Atlantic Ocean. In 2010, he played for his **national team** and for a team in England. Honduras and England are more than 5,000 miles (8,046 kilometers) apart.

Maynor Figueroa plays for his English team.

Shoe Box

The soccer collection on these pages belongs to the authors. It shows some of the top Central American stars.

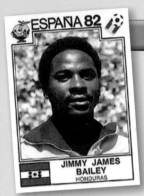

Jimmy Bailey

Forward • Honduras
Jimmy Bailey scored the goal that got Honduras into the 1982 **World Cup**.

Magico Gonzalez

Striker • El Salvador
Some say Magico Gonzalez was the greatest player ever from Central America.

Rolando Fonseca

Striker • Costa Rica
Rolando Fonseca loved to score goals on long shots.

Amado Guevara

Midfielder • Honduras
Amado Guevara was a star in Central America, Europe, and the United States.

Carlos Ruiz

Forward • Guatemala
Fans called Carlos Ruiz the "Little Fish." He was fast and hard to handle.

Maynor Figueroa

Defender • Honduras
Maynor Figueroa had a powerful left leg.

Osael Romero

Midfielder • El Salvador
Osael Romero scored goals with quick shots.

Marco Pappa

Midfielder • Guatemala
Marco Pappa beat teams with hard shots and great passes.

Can't Touch This

In soccer, sometimes the ball is kicked high in the air. When this happens, players use their heads to make a pass or take a shot. Only goalkeepers are allowed to touch the ball with their arms and hands.

Costa Rica's Silvia Betancourt tries a "header."

Walter Centeno of Costa Rica prepares for a direct kick.

16

Just For Kicks

Watching soccer is more fun when you know some of the rules:

- There are two kinds of **free kicks** in soccer.

- On a Direct Kick, players can try to score a goal.

- On an Indirect Kick, the ball must touch another player first.

On the Map

Girls and boys play soccer all over Central America:

1. Belize
2. Costa Rica
3. El Salvador
4. Guatemala

5. Honduras
6. Nicaragua
7. Panama

25 CTS. COSTA RICA CORREO AEREO ROMA 1960

2 Costa Rica

BELIZE
$2 +1
PRO-SPORTS

1 Belize

La Copa Mundial 1930 URUGUAY 4 ARGENTINA MOMENTOS DE GLORIA 1 Cts NICARAGUA

6 Nicaragua

Many countries have their own soccer stamps!

19

Stop Action

Priscilla Tapia of Costa Rica is the goalkeeper.

Goalkeepers wear special uniforms.

The net stops the ball after a goal.

Soccer shoes are also called "boots."

We Won!

Central America has some of the best teams in the world!

Men's Soccer	CONCACAF* Champion	CONCACAF Runner-Up
Costa Rica	1963,1969, & 1989	2002
Guatemala	1967	1965 & 1969
Honduras	1981	1985 & 1991
El Salvador		1963 & 1981
Panama		2005

Women's Soccer	CONCACAF 3rd Place	CONCACAF 4th Place
Costa Rica	1998	2002 & 2010
Guatemala		1998

* CONCACAF stands for Confederation of North, Central American, and Caribbean Association Football. It is made up of national teams from these regions.

Panama's players and fans celebrate in 2005.

Soccer Words

FREE KICKS
Shots given to a team after a foul has been called.

LEAGUES
Groups of teams that compete against each other.

NATIONAL TEAM
A team made up of players from the same country.

WORLD CUP
The tournament that decides the world champion of soccer. The World Cup is played every four years.

Index

Photos are on **bold** numbered pages.

Learn More

Learn more about the World Cup at www.fifa.com

Learn more about men's soccer at www.mlssoccer.com

Learn more about women's soccer at www.womensprosoccer.com